Prosperity

Prosperity

Felicha Vaughn

THE REGENCY
PUBLISHERS

Copyright © 2022 Felicha Vaughn.

All rights reserved. No part of this book may be reproduced in any form or by any electronic or mechanical means, including information storage and retrieval systems, without permission in writing from the author and publisher, except by reviewers, who may quote brief passages in a review.

ISBN: 978-1-959434-82-5 (Paperback Edition)
ISBN: 978-1-959434-83-2 (Hardcover Edition)
ISBN: 978-1-959434-81-8 (E-book Edition)

Book Ordering Information

The Regency Publishers, US
521 5th Ave 17th floor NY, NY10175

Phone Number: (315)537-3088 ext 1007
Email: info@theregencypublishers.com
www.theregencypublishers.com

Printed in the United States of America

Contents

Biography vii
Acknowledgment ix

Name 1
Walking 2
Sunday Morning 3
Bright 4
Night 5
Wedding Date 6
Jesus 7
Spending time 8
Planning 9
Sing 10
Color 11
Every Morning 12
Christmas 13
Valentine's Day 14
Summer 15
Decide 16
Praying 17
Winter 18
School 19
House 20
File 21
Together 22
Studying 23
Christmas 24
Mother 25

Jesus Name	26
Writing	27
Start	28
Sing	29
Psalm	30
Lord	31
Living	32
Year	33
Fall	34
Breathe	35
Crisp	36
December	37
Father's Day	38
Mathew	39
Holy Spirit	40
Goodness	41
Family	42
Church	43
Bible	44
Genesis	45
Feed	46
Change	47
Joy	48
Apple	49
Trend	50
Watching	51
Holy Spirit	52
Husband	53

Biography

My name is Felicha Vaughn and for many years I have been thinking about the way I have forsaken the way as I have spent the way. As a parent, I have to show respect for myself and the answer is there in the bible it said so not like your heart be trouble. I enjoy the thing I do for a living so I write poem time to come. I have three kids and a husband.

Acknowledgment

The Book of Prosperity is a Christian book that people love to read. In the name of Jesus, we continue to pray every day and every night. When u read the book it is inspired people to read the Bible every day and for years to come.

Name

In the name of Jesus we as firm believers, stand together. We as people, come to church every week to study god work. That afternoon, I went to see my Pastor for Christian advice on my Mother and Father and my Family to come together as a unity in the book of Mathew Chapter 6 Verse 6 reads to go to your prayer and closet and pray and study good work.

Walking

Walking thu the body of the valley of Christ where I sing in the choir. My parents took us to church every Wednesday and Sunday. We have to learn from the lord Darkness comes from the light trusting our hearts we have to learn for ourselves in the name of Jesus.

Sunday Morning

My family decided to have Sunday Morning breakfast with my Grandparents. We all went to Church together at 11:00 am. My sister went to go to the store before we decided to go to Church. When she was in the store she saw a $5 Dollar bill on the floor. When she saw it on the floor she gave it to the Cashier. When she did she went back in the car with her family. The Cashier gave the money to the Young lady she bought some gas for her family to go home.

Bright

It was a bright sunny day. I decide to go to the Beach and relax. When I did I saw a shark in the water. It was headed my way. I got up and ran as fast as I can. I scream and yell at the same time. Two hours later my daughter asked me she said that her mother wants wrong. I told her I said that I see a Shark in the water. We decided to call a lifeguard. He came to the Beach took a gun and kill it.

Night

We decided to gather for prayer in the name of Jesus at my sister's house on a school night. The people we met in the park came to the door and knocked. We make the decision to bring a bible. In the house, we added more space. We collected money for the church's collection. We raise enough money to rebuild the church, purchase new hymnals, and purchase pews.

Wedding Date

My parents told us that they were renewing their vows. Their wedding date has been planned for December 17. 50 years have passed since they got married. They have 10 grandchildren and 5 children. My mother was a powerful woman. She maintained the family's unity. I served as the maid of honor for the nuptials. My parents have recently renewed their vows. They visited Jamaica for their honeymoon. They spend a week there. We arrange a surprise party for them when they return while they are on their honeymoon.

Jesus

Jesus Name is the son of Joseph and Mary.Jesus was born on Christmas day. We celebrate on Christmas day by receive gifts for the kids and we can come over there to see if they can get some more gifts. Just for your information went out to get the name of Jesus Christ.

Spending time

When I was 7 years old, I decided to go to my aunt's house to spend the night with her. She says yes and my mother fixes my overnight bag. When I came to my aunt's house, she show me my bedroom. I like my room. I saw my cousin's picture on the wall. She came into the room, sat beside me and she told me that my cousin lives in California and doing a modeling job. Later that day we read the bible and we pray God before I went to bed.

Planning

We are planning a trip to Nevada where we are going to see a football game. In the hot weather. In the hot weather under the 95-degree temperature, we got there. We saw a lot of people sitting on our seats, we ask them if these seats are ours and then we got some food in the first inning. My grandson caught the ball when it started to rain. We had to leave in the third quarter and go back to our room, pray and study our bible in Jesus name.

Sing

As we sing to the word of the lord we continue to love each other when we pray to each other for our sick and shut-in walking in the valley of love. To love ourselves each and every day and going to church every week makes me want to sing every day.

Color

We pray for you and your family in the name of Jesus, and we count it a privilege to go back to the church and pray with you there. The color of the picture looks so much better on the wall since it is the color of Jesus Christ.

Every Morning

We made the decision to visit the church and pray. Today, we are going to purchase extra food so that we may come back later and get more drinks to go with our meal. My parents are going to go shopping for our kids' school outfits. This afternoon, I'm going to go walking right after I get off of work.

Christmas

Christmas is once every year. The birth of Christ was birth on December 25. Every year we celebrated this day. Every year children sleep when Santa brings gifts to every door and every child lives on the road. It brightens my day to see the kids receive their gifts.

Valentine's Day

Roses are red, violets are blue, we love you, we do for you. In the name of Jesus Christ, we continue to pray for our sick and homebound. Sending Valentine cards to our loved ones makes them feel extra special at this time of year. Valentine's Day occurs once a month.

Summer

Summertime is my favorite season. I love going to the beach and building sandcastles with the kids. In the name of Jesus, we pray for our loved ones that they have the time of their life.

Decide

We made the decision to travel outside the country. We were going to spend a week in Canada, so we went to get our passports and buy some Walgreens. We packed up, left on a Thursday afternoon, and invited my parents to join us. Two hours later, my mother called and said she didn't want us to go on the trip because she had seen my husband on the phone talking to his mother. She informed him that she had been notified by the doctor that she had cancer at stage 4. We had to cancel our trip in the name of Jesus, she said.

Praying

I graduated on May 17 and placed in the top 10 of my class. I would read the Bible and find the relevant passages before I started studying for the test. In the mighty name of Jesus, put God first. The Bible is full of wisdom, love, courage, and trust. Only put your faith in God. I want to read every day because I go to church and read the Bible every day.

Winter

My mother came knocking on our door one chilly winter day. When she arrived at the house, I immediately sensed a problem. She admitted to us that she was late on her rent. The landlord claims that she is unable to pay the rent and will be required to vacate the property in 30 days. The following day, we went to the bank and withdrew the necessary funds to pay her rent for the ensuing years and prevent her from being evicted from her apartment.

School

When I was young I didn't like school at first. As years went by I understand it better. I became a book writer. I went to college to pick up my education. My professor taught me to write an essay. About writing, I go well when I write my first book. Studying the bible, teach me more about the Holy Spirit.

House

On a winter night, we were all in bed sleep. All of a sudden we heard a loud sound outside. My father get up from the bed and he saw a deer running inside the house. We all run away to the living room. He called animal control, and ten minutes later the man came to get the deer out of the house. There was no one hurt and we decide to go back to bed and get some help.

File

Our daughter asked me to go to the hospital for the remainder of the day so that we could come over there for me. Dominique is the best employee at the hospital. She works 8 hours per day. She wants to go to the hospital and get some more tests done. Daryl Jr. is our first son, and Antwon is our youngest son.

Together

Coming together as one body of the day. We are doing well. Touch the name of Jesus we pray every morning before we go out and get some rest. I gave the kids and I will be there for at least one day and then we can go back and get some sleep. The next day comes in the name of Jesus we pray every day before we go back and get some rest. Praying together as well as we get together and pray about the name and your family is the time to come and receive it.

Studying

Going back to school is the best thing I have ever done. Studying hair makes me want more people to see me as they want me to do their hair as a client every week. I work 3 hours per week part-time. Giving back to Jesus gives me pleasure to future my bible studies in church and at home as well.

Christmas

One time of the year, usually around Christmas, my kids get their presents. Annual visits to my mother are made. Christmas supper is prepared by her. She set up Christmas for when Santa visits the living room and we open our presents on Christmas.

Mother

Every year, we have a celebration for mothers. Although being a mother of three has not always been simple, I have always remained a constant in their lives. 11 grandchildren and 5 children make up my mother's family. When we most needed her, she maintained the family. We gave mom a mother's day ring with five birthday stones from the five of us on that special day. We appreciate everything that our mother does.

Jesus Name

In the name of Jesus, we pray for our sick and shut-in Mathew Chapter 6 Verse 6, go to the prayer closet and pray about it. Faith is the strongest word in the bible. Wisdom courage is in the Bible.

Writing

The remainder of the week was spent writing a novel until day's end. With the other kids in the English Class, I am taking a class at school. This afternoon, about 5:30 PM, I'm going for a walk. I tried my best, but it was nice to see you and your family. Writing a book requires a significant amount of time.

Start

My family and I plan a trip to New York City, and when we got there we see the empire state building. We visited our relative in Brooklyn. My husband has a relative who lives there, they started school in September. When we first started dating I went to New York for the first time, I was nervous. I went back for the second time and we took our child and went to Queen; Bronx and Manhattan.

Sing

Sing to the Dr. Office she said she was going to be there at least once. The girl in the name of her house playing with my mom and her dad. Touching the other one is the best time to come over there and get some sleep. The babysitter and your mom are going to be there around the same time as well. Sing in the name of the day she was going to be by her mom's house playing with my friends. Singing and your family at the park and your house and she said she would like more than I am going walking around the same time as she is. Praise to the Dr Office and your family you are doing great your family is going to have to get together with me for the courgment and the beautiful picture always made me feel better thank u for telling me that you are welcome.

Psalm

In the book of Psalms in the name of Jesus Christ. The best way to get my second one is the best time for me to come over there for the rest of the day. Sing in the morning and every night before we leave the house and get some time for you. Thinking of you and your family and friends with the place and the beautiful family is the best time for me to come over there and get some more praise and worship together.

Lord

Let us pray about the day and then we can go from there. Touching our loved ones is the best time to come to the house and get some rest of the day. Going to church every week and then we can come over there for the weekend and get some more praise and worship. Giving thanks for the courgment and the rest of the day and then we can come over there for the day and then we can go back and see what they have to do with the kids.

Living

Living in the same area as well and your family. Truly I say to you and your family were the same time as we was praying for you. The people can be there at the park and the weather is good for us. We are doing better today and I have a safe day at the house playing with my Grand babies today. Living in the same town when you receive the email and I will be there around the same time as you can come over there for me.

Year

On that day of the year, we are welcome to visit for the remainder of the day. It was nice to see you and your family, and today we can go over there so I can come to your home and pray for you. We can go to church every week, and after that, we can go over there for us and then we can go back to the house and pray. Through the years, we have been able to take care of us and our family.

Fall

On that day of the year, we are welcome to visit for the remainder of the day. It was nice to see you and your family, and today we can go over there so I can come to your home and pray for you. We can go to church every week, and after that, we can go over there for us and then we can go back to the house and pray. Through the years, we have been able to take care of us and our family.

Breathe

Breathe in, breathe out when you take breath classes in college. CPR are class's college courses where you can get some credit in class. We decided to go out to eat with our family. We had just had our dinner. Five minutes later we saw someone just got choked on their food. I with over to their table and I can come over there to help.

Crisp

Crisp is the best way to get my second one is a good day for me to come to the house. Halloween is October 31 every year I see kids outside with their outfits on Trick or Treat. We made Rice Crispy treats for Halloween Night.

December

My son's birthday is in December. Daryl Jr. will be 30 on December 3. He was born on his grandfather's birthday. Daryl and I got married on December 18. We sing Christmas carols all year round. We go to my mother's on Christmas day.

Father's Day

On Father's Day today, I was going on a date with my husband. Our Father and I will get it done when we are doing it today. My Father is my best friend and we can come over there for me. Search days and I will be there at about the same time as well as I. My Father has 10 brothers and sisters. My Father has been together as one body and the beautiful picture always has made me feel better thank God for me to come to the house. Touching lives in the name of Jesus we are good to see you and your family and friends.

Mathew

Mathew is in the new chapter of the bible. I like the book of Mathew because it teaches me to read the bible and study good work. Mathew, Mark, Luke, and John those books are in the New Testament. Mark chapter 11 verses 22 read and answer and said have faith in God. Faith is the strongest word in the bible. Chapter 3 verse 16 for God so loved the world he gave his only son. Reading the bible study God's word put God first.

Holy Spirit

Going to church every week and then we can come over there and get some more praise and worship together. Come together with the kids and we can come over to the church and see what they have to offer. I believe in the Holy Spirit. Every morning and every night before we leave the house.

Goodness

Goodness from someone's heart is someone's love. Coming together as one is the time together as one. Touching, Loving, and Caring is the way we need to spend time together. Going to school for nursing is the way that we need to take time to make time for each other, coming together as people to share our lives in the name of Jesus Christ. Reading the way we wanted to be treated spiritually. Singing to one another is the way we wanted to be.

Family

Spending time with our family is the way we wanted to spend with them. Touching live with one another is the way it was meant to be. Family time in unity is together. My family spent time with our loved ones. We have a family reunion once a year. We live out of town. I love my family with all my heart and soul. I see them when I have the chance.

Church

I love going to church every week. I sing with the church. We have a lot of singing and praising music in the church. Praying in the church is the way we have. The pastor read the bible and teaches good work. We have ministries work for the children's choir. Searching for the goodness of someone's love we praise the love and love them as if we have to come together as a family.

Bible

Reading the Bible every day and studying good work is the way we like to read the bible. In the book of Hebrews, Chapter 11 talks about Faith. Faith is a strong word in the bible. Studying reading work with the bible teaches us motivation with the work. In the name of Jesus, we can continue to come together in men groups in the church. Study god's work shows us and teaches us the way we need to come together as a family.

Genesis

Genesis is the first book in the bible. Reading a book gives us the pleasure to know what we need to study is a book. Coming together to show the book of Genesis, we need to show what we are to study what the word is about. There are 66 books in the bible. I like the king James book. I have a bible in the house, I read it every morning before I go out the door. Remember study work for the lord himself, as if we know him all our lives.

Feed

I have been fed by the word of the lord himself. Coming together as a family continues to show the way we need to. I have been by the word myself in the way I need to be. On a warm day, I decided to go to the park. When I was there, I saw two people there. I ask them, "Have you eaten lunch" and they say no. We decided that we would go to McDonald's for lunch. When we were there, we saw a man and he didn't have enough money to pay for his lunch. It says in the bible; when some are hungry, feed them. When someone is thirsty, give them something to drink. We pray, we study and we give them the bible to study.

Change

We determined that a day in the park would be enjoyable. I'll be at the church about noon while the weather is still warm and there is more praise and worship. Thank you for the encouragement and the lovely photo, which always makes me feel better. We can hold yard sales again soon.

Joy

Joy to the world the lord has come. "J" means Jesus Christ. "O" means observing and doing the lord's work. "Y" means the Yellow color of Christ to the world. Touching the lives where we have to love our friends and our loved ones. On Wednesday night, we have to come together as one. In the name of Jesus, we continue to lift our hands on him. I went to my friend's house to see how she is doing, and come to find out she was going to his sister's house and praying because she just need a prayer to lift her spirit up in Jesus's name.

Apple

My favorite fruit is the apple. They are available in three different colors: Red, Yellow, and Green. I cook a pie once a week and enjoy the color green. I bake for Daryl once a week. In October, we can also transform them into candied apples. Once a year, I witness children trick-or-treating at churches. I think a car painted in the color sweet apple red looks lovely. I enjoy the fall season because the leaves become lovely shades of red and yellow.

Trend

The trend went the name of what we have gone by what we said, Thank you. Coming together as, a family we pray, laughed, and enjoy each other company. This year went by fast, Thank you Jesus for giving me the knowledge to write a book. It takes courage and wisdom in the name of Jesus.

Watching

I was watching T.V. on Sunday afternoon, I had it on the news where gas prices people goes on vacation. I would love to go to Atlanta just to visit and see the real live life game. I would love to love to comeback someday.

Holy Spirit

The Holy Spirit is the power feeling when you put God first. When you study good work, you need to study every day. Come together as one we can relate to each other together. Listening to the pastor makes me want to study the bible more. I always remember when we put God first studied him first pray and started our day and at night.

Husband

My husband and I been married for thirty-three and half years, we celebrated our wedding renewal on July 11, 2021. A year later we celebrate that day. We have three kids; Dominique, Daryl Jr., and Antwon. Antwon's birthday is October 23 and he will turn 25.

www.ingramcontent.com/pod-product-compliance
Lightning Source LLC
LaVergne TN
LVHW020437080526
838202LV00055B/5234